WORSHIP & PRAYER JOURNAL

·····················

At the Feet of Jesus

Record Your Time As You Sit at the Feet of Jesus.

CHRISTINA PERERA

THIS BOOK BELONGS TO:

....

_____

Let God Arise & His Enemies Scatter

Oh, magnify the LORD with me, And let us exalt His name together.
Psalm 34:3 NKJV

Something powerful happens when we worship the Lord Jesus. We enter His gates with thanksgiving and praise for who He is and what He has done for us. The Bible declares that as we worship, He fights our enemies whether they are sickness, wrong mindsets, or other hindrances.

As you sit at Jesus' feet, your faith will grow as you hear His word, commune with Him in prayer, and feast upon His faithfulness.

Use this journal to record your time with God. You can use each section for a day or a week depending on your schedule. Each week/day section includes places to record the scriptures you are reading, what you see in the scripture, your response in prayer and a journaling page. Record answered prayers in the back section. Don't forget to grab your colored pencils and get creative with the images.

I hope this journal will serve as a powerful memorial of your relationship with a living, loving Savior.

GRAB YOUR BIBLE AND LET'S GET STARTED ...

JOURNAL SECTION

· ·

At the Feet of Jesus

Record Your Time As You Sit at the Feet of Jesus.

Color Me

Scripture:

_____

_____

_____

_____

Vision:

_____

_____

_____

_____

Response:

_____

_____

_____

_____

Journal Page

Record what Jesus is speaking to your heart.

Date:_____

Color Me

_____

_____

_____

_____

_____

_____

_____

_____

_____

_____

_____

_____

_____

_____

WEEK/DAY_____

. . . .

Color Me

Scripture:

_____

_____

_____

_____

Vision:

_____

_____

_____

_____

Response:

_____

_____

_____

_____

Journal Page

Record what Jesus is speaking to your heart.

Date:_____

_____

_____

_____

_____

_____

_____

_____

_____

_____

_____

_____

_____

_____

WEEK/DAY_____

· · · · · · · · · · · · · · · · · · · ·

Color Me

Scripture:

_____
_____
_____
_____

Vision:

_____
_____
_____
_____

Response:

_____
_____
_____

Journal Page

Record what Jesus is speaking to your heart.

Date:_____

· · · · · · · · · · · · · · · · · · · ·

Color Me

Scripture:

_____

_____

_____

_____

Vision:

_____

_____

_____

_____

Response:

_____

_____

_____

_____

Journal Page

Record what Jesus is speaking to your heart.

Date:_____

_____

_____

_____

_____

_____

_____

_____

_____

_____

_____

_____

_____

_____

Color Me

Scripture:

_____
_____
_____
_____

Vision:

_____
_____
_____
_____

Response:

_____
_____
_____
_____

Journal Page

Record what Jesus is speaking to your heart.

Date:_____

_____

_____

_____

_____

_____

_____

_____

_____

_____

_____

_____

_____

_____

_____

WEEK/DAY_____

· · · · · · · · · · · · · · · · · · · ·

Color Me

Scripture:

_____

_____

_____

_____

Vision:

_____

_____

_____

_____

Response:

_____

_____

_____

_____

Journal Page

Record what Jesus is speaking to your heart.

Date:_____

Color Me

Scripture: _____
_____
_____
_____

Vision: _____
_____
_____
_____

Response: _____
_____
_____
_____

Journal Page

Record what Jesus is speaking to your heart.

Date:_____

_____

_____

_____

_____

_____

_____

_____

_____

_____

_____

_____

_____

_____

_____

_____

· · · · · · · · · · · · · · · · · · ·

Color Me

Scripture:

_____

_____

_____

_____

Vision:

_____

_____

_____

_____

Response:

_____

_____

_____

_____

Journal Page

Record what Jesus is speaking to your heart.

Date:_____

_____

_____

_____

_____

_____

_____

_____

_____

_____

_____

_____

_____

_____

_____

Color Me

Scripture:

_____
_____
_____
_____

Vision:

_____
_____
_____
_____

Response:

_____
_____
_____
_____

Journal Page

Record what Jesus is speaking to your heart.

Date:_____

· · · · · · · · · · · · · · · · · · ·

Color Me

Scripture:

_____

_____

_____

_____

Vision:

_____

_____

_____

_____

Response:

_____

_____

_____

_____

Journal Page

Record what Jesus is speaking to your heart.

Date:_____

· · · · · · · · · · · · · · · · · · ·

Color Me

Scripture:

_____
_____
_____
_____

Vision:

_____
_____
_____
_____

Response:

_____
_____
_____
_____

Journal Page

Record what Jesus is speaking to your heart.

Date:_____

WEEK/DAY _____

. . . .

Color Me

Scripture:

_____

_____

_____

_____

Vision:

_____

_____

_____

_____

Response:

_____

_____

_____

Journal Page

Record what Jesus is speaking to your heart.

*Date:*_____

· · · · · · · · · · · · · · · · · · · ·

Color Me

Scripture:

_____

_____

_____

_____

Vision:

_____

_____

_____

_____

Response:

_____

_____

_____

_____

Journal Page

Record what Jesus is speaking to your heart.

Date:_____

· · · · · · · · · · · · · · · · · · · ·

Color Me

Scripture:

_____

_____

_____

_____

Vision:

_____

_____

_____

_____

Response:

_____

_____

_____

_____

Journal Page

Record what Jesus is speaking to your heart.

*Date:*_____

_____

_____

_____

_____

_____

_____

_____

_____

_____

_____

_____

_____

_____

_____

Color Me

Scripture:

_____

_____

_____

_____

Vision:

_____

_____

_____

_____

Response:

_____

_____

_____

_____

Journal Page

Record what Jesus is speaking to your heart.

Date:_____

· ·

Color Me

Scripture:

_____

_____

_____

_____

Vision:

_____

_____

_____

_____

Response:

_____

_____

_____

_____

Journal Page

Record what Jesus is speaking to your heart.

Date:_____

Color Me

Scripture:

_____

_____

_____

_____

Vision:

_____

_____

_____

_____

Response:

_____

_____

_____

Journal Page

Record what Jesus is speaking to your heart.

Date:_____

_____

_____

_____

_____

_____

_____

_____

_____

_____

_____

_____

_____

_____

_____

_____

_____

_____

Color Me

Scripture:

_____

_____

_____

_____

Vision:

_____

_____

_____

_____

Response:

_____

_____

_____

_____

Journal Page

Record what Jesus is speaking to your heart.

Date:_____

. . . .

Color Me

Scripture:

_____
_____
_____
_____

Vision:

_____
_____
_____
_____

Response:

_____
_____
_____
_____

Journal Page

Record what Jesus is speaking to your heart.

Date:_____

_____

_____

_____

_____

_____

_____

_____

_____

_____

_____

_____

_____

_____

_____

WEEK/DAY_____

. . . .

Color Me

Scripture:

_____

_____

_____

_____

Vision:

_____

_____

_____

_____

Response:

_____

_____

_____

_____

Journal Page

Record what Jesus is speaking to your heart.

Date:_____

WEEK/DAY_____

· · · · · · · · · · · · · · · · · · ·

Color Me

Scripture:

_____

_____

_____

_____

Vision:

_____

_____

_____

_____

Response:

_____

_____

_____

_____

Journal Page

Record what Jesus is speaking to your heart.

Date:_____

Color Me

Scripture:

_____

_____

_____

Vision:

_____

_____

_____

Response:

_____

_____

_____

Journal Page

Record what Jesus is speaking to your heart.

Date:_____

_____

_____

_____

_____

_____

_____

_____

_____

_____

_____

_____

_____

_____

_____

_____

WEEK/DAY_____

· · · · · · · · · · · · · · · · · · · ·

Color Me

Scripture:

_____
_____
_____
_____

Vision:

_____
_____
_____
_____

Response:

_____
_____
_____
_____

Journal Page

Record what Jesus is speaking to your heart.

Date:_____

_____

_____

_____

_____

_____

_____

_____

_____

_____

_____

_____

_____

_____

_____

WEEK/DAY_____

· ·

Color Me

Scripture:

_____

_____

_____

_____

Vision:

_____

_____

_____

_____

Response:

_____

_____

_____

_____

Journal Page

Record what Jesus is speaking to your heart.

Date:_____

_____

_____

_____

_____

_____

_____

_____

_____

_____

_____

_____

_____

_____

_____

Color Me

Scripture:

_____
_____
_____
_____

Vision:

_____
_____
_____
_____

Response:

_____
_____
_____
_____

Journal Page

Record what Jesus is speaking to your heart.

Date:_____

. . . .

Color Me

Scripture:

_____

_____

_____

_____

Vision:

_____

_____

_____

_____

Response:

_____

_____

_____

_____

Journal Page

Record what Jesus is speaking to your heart.

Date:_____

_____

_____

_____

_____

_____

_____

_____

_____

_____

_____

_____

_____

_____

_____

WEEK/DAY_____

· · · · · · · · · · · · · · · · · · ·

Color Me

Scripture:

_____

_____

_____

_____

Vision:

_____

_____

_____

_____

Response:

_____

_____

_____

Journal Page

Record what Jesus is speaking to your heart.

Date:_____

_____

_____

_____

_____

_____

_____

_____

_____

_____

_____

_____

_____

_____

_____

_____

WEEK/DAY________

Color Me

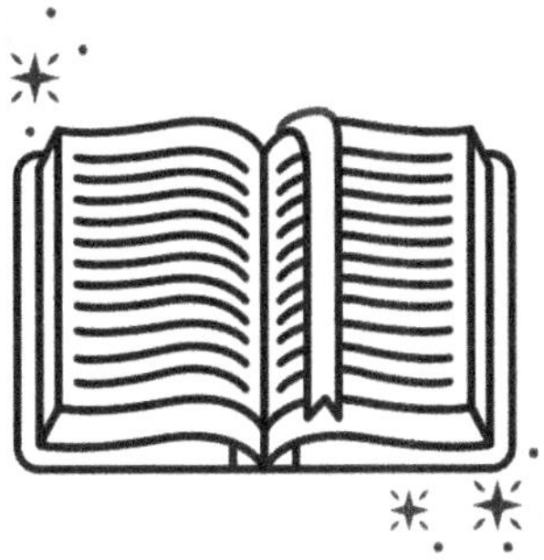

Scripture:

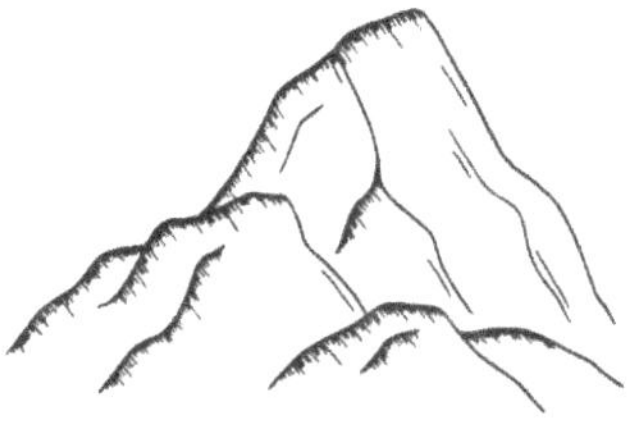

Vision:

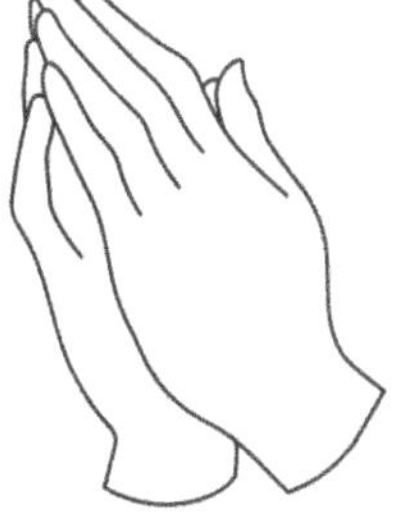

Response:

Journal Page

Record what Jesus is speaking to your heart.

Date:_____

· · · · · · · · · · · · · · · · · · ·

Color Me

Scripture:

_____

_____

_____

_____

Vision:

_____

_____

_____

_____

Response:

_____

_____

_____

Journal Page

Record what Jesus is speaking to your heart.

Date:_____

Color Me

Scripture:

_____
_____
_____
_____

Vision:

_____
_____
_____
_____

Response:

_____
_____
_____
_____

Journal Page

Record what Jesus is speaking to your heart.

Date:_____

WEEK/DAY_____

· · · · · · · · · · · · · · · · · · ·

Color Me

Scripture:

_____
_____
_____
_____

Vision:

_____
_____
_____
_____

Response:

_____
_____
_____

Journal Page

Record what Jesus is speaking to your heart.

Date:_____

_____

_____

_____

_____

_____

_____

_____

_____

_____

_____

_____

_____

_____

_____

Color Me

Scripture: _____

_____

_____

_____

Vision: _____

_____

_____

_____

Response: _____

_____

_____

_____

Journal Page

Record what Jesus is speaking to your heart.

Date:_____

· ·

Color Me

Scripture:

_____

_____

_____

_____

Vision:

_____

_____

_____

_____

Response:

_____

_____

_____

_____

Journal Page

Record what Jesus is speaking to your heart.

*Date:*_____

_____

_____

_____

_____

_____

_____

_____

_____

_____

_____

_____

_____

_____

_____

Color Me

Scripture:
_____
_____
_____
_____

Vision:
_____
_____
_____
_____

Response:
_____
_____
_____
_____

Journal Page

Record what Jesus is speaking to your heart.

Date:_____

· · · · · · · · · · · · · · · · · · · ·

Color Me

Scripture:

_____

_____

_____

_____

Vision:

_____

_____

_____

_____

Response:

_____

_____

_____

_____

Journal Page

Record what Jesus is speaking to your heart.

Date:_____

. . . .

Color Me

Scripture:

_____

_____

_____

_____

Vision:

_____

_____

_____

_____

Response:

_____

_____

_____

_____

Journal Page

Record what Jesus is speaking to your heart.

Date:_____

· · · · · · · · · · · · · · · · · · · ·

Color Me

Scripture:

_____

_____

_____

_____

Vision:

_____

_____

_____

_____

Response:

_____

_____

_____

_____

Journal Page

Record what Jesus is speaking to your heart.

Date:_____

WEEK/DAY ________

Color Me

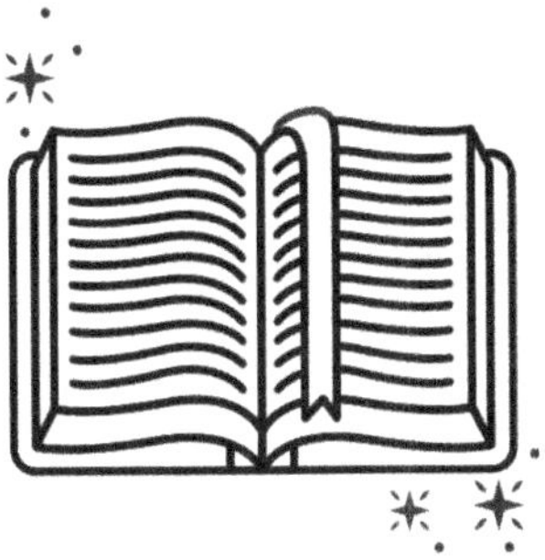

Scripture:

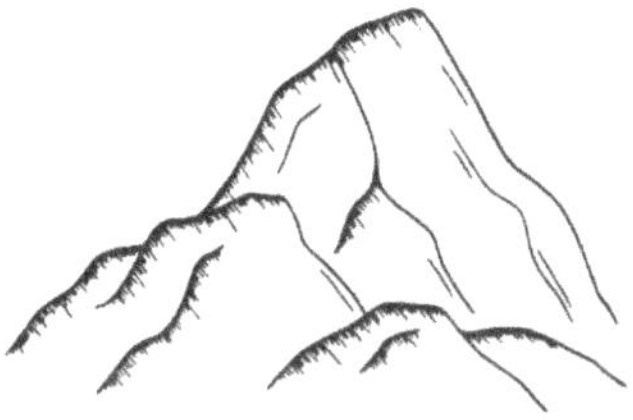

Vision:

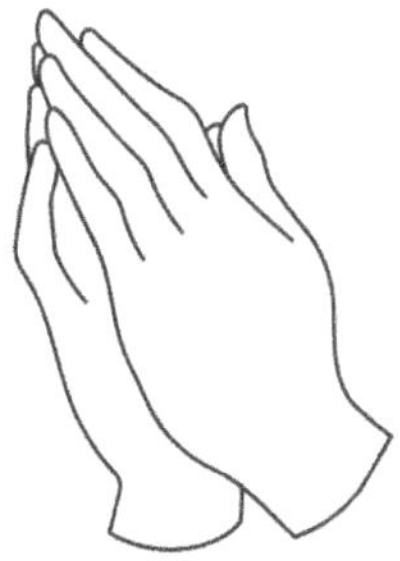

Response:

Journal Page

Record what Jesus is speaking to your heart.

Date:_____

_____

_____

_____

_____

_____

_____

_____

_____

_____

_____

_____

_____

_____

_____

Color Me

Scripture:

Vision:

Response:

Journal Page

Record what Jesus is speaking to your heart.

Date:_____

WEEK/DAY _____

· ·

Color Me

Scripture:

_____

_____

_____

_____

Vision:

_____

_____

_____

_____

Response:

_____

_____

_____

_____

Journal Page

Record what Jesus is speaking to your heart.

Date:_____

Color Me

Scripture:

_____
_____
_____
_____

Vision:

_____
_____
_____
_____

Response:

_____
_____
_____
_____

Journal Page

Record what Jesus is speaking to your heart.

Date:_____

_____

_____

_____

_____

_____

_____

_____

_____

_____

_____

_____

_____

_____

_____

_____

WEEK/DAY_____

. . . .

Color Me

Scripture:

_____

_____

_____

_____

Vision:

_____

_____

_____

_____

Response:

_____

_____

_____

_____

Journal Page

Record what Jesus is speaking to your heart.

Date:_____

_____

_____

_____

_____

_____

_____

_____

_____

_____

_____

_____

_____

_____

_____

Color Me

Scripture:

_____

_____

_____

_____

Vision:

_____

_____

_____

_____

Response:

_____

_____

_____

_____

Journal Page

Record what Jesus is speaking to your heart.

Date:_____

_____

_____

_____

_____

_____

_____

_____

_____

_____

_____

_____

_____

_____

Color Me

Scripture:

_____
_____
_____
_____

Vision:

_____
_____
_____
_____

Response:

_____
_____
_____
_____

Journal Page

Record what Jesus is speaking to your heart.

Date:_____

· · · · · · · · · · · · · · · · · · ·

Color Me

Scripture:

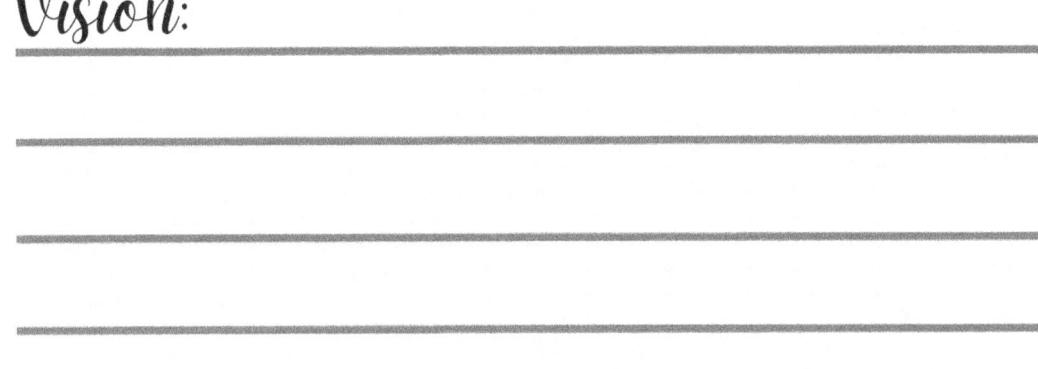

Vision:

Response:

Journal Page

Record what Jesus is speaking to your heart.

Date:_____

WEEK/DAY _____

· · · · · · · · · · · · · · · · · ·

Color Me

Scripture:

_____

_____

_____

_____

Vision:

_____

_____

_____

_____

Response:

_____

_____

_____

_____

Journal Page

Record what Jesus is speaking to your heart.

Date:_____

WEEK/DAY_____

Color Me

Scripture:

_____

_____

_____

_____

Vision:

_____

_____

_____

_____

Response:

_____

_____

_____

Journal Page

Record what Jesus is speaking to your heart.

Date:_____

_____

_____

_____

_____

_____

_____

_____

_____

_____

_____

_____

_____

_____

· · · · · · · · · · · · · · · · · · · ·

Color Me

Scripture:

_____

_____

_____

_____

Vision:

_____

_____

_____

_____

Response:

_____

_____

_____

_____

Journal Page

Record what Jesus is speaking to your heart.

Date:_____

_____

_____

_____

_____

_____

_____

_____

_____

_____

_____

_____

_____

_____

_____

_____

WEEK/DAY _____

· · · · · · · · · · · · · · · · · ·

Color Me

Scripture:

_____

_____

_____

_____

Vision:

_____

_____

_____

_____

Response:

_____

_____

_____

_____

Journal Page

Record what Jesus is speaking to your heart.

Date:_____

_____

_____

_____

_____

_____

_____

_____

_____

_____

_____

_____

_____

_____

WEEK/DAY __________

Color Me

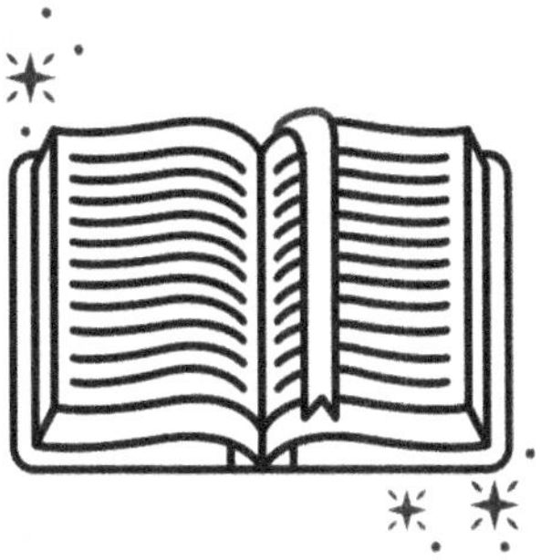

Scripture:

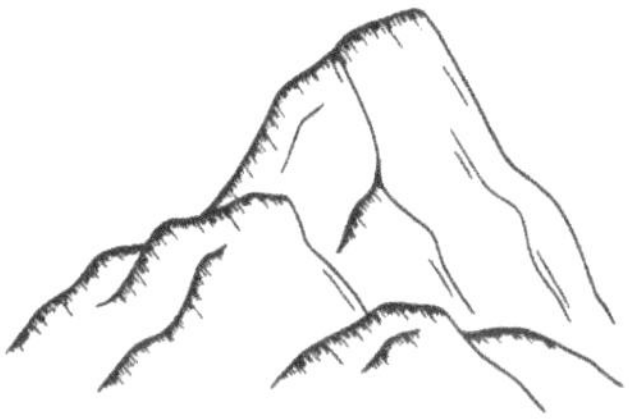

Vision:

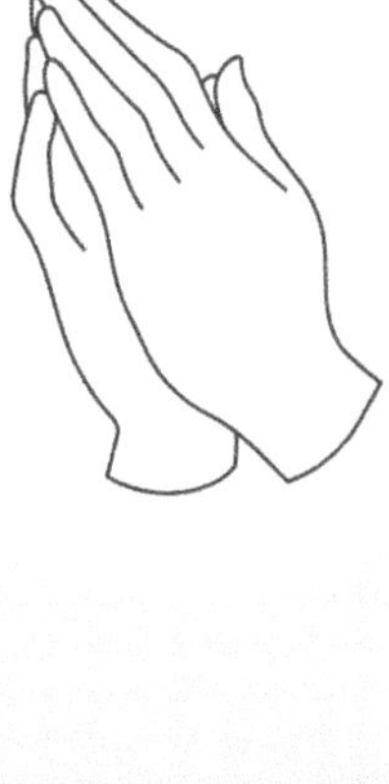

Response:

Journal Page

Record what Jesus is speaking to your heart.

Date:_____

Color Me

Scripture:

_____
_____
_____
_____

Vision:

_____
_____
_____
_____

revdpeterson@icloud.com

Response:

_____
_____
_____
_____

Journal Page

Record what Jesus is speaking to your heart.

Date:_____

_____

_____

_____

_____

_____

_____

_____

_____

_____

_____

_____

_____

_____

. . . .

Color Me

Scripture:

_____

_____

_____

_____

Vision:

_____

_____

_____

_____

Response:

_____

_____

_____

_____

Journal Page

Record what Jesus is speaking to your heart.

Date:_____

_____

_____

_____

_____

_____

_____

_____

_____

_____

_____

_____

_____

_____

_____

ANSWERED PRAYERS SECTION

....

At the Feet of Jesus

Record Your Time As You Sit at the Feet of Jesus.

Answered Prayers

*These milestones are essential to remember as you continue
to believe for God's promises to manifest in your life.*

_____

_____

_____

_____

_____

_____

_____

_____

_____

_____

_____

Answered Prayers

These milestones are essential to remember as you continue to believe for God's promises to manifest in your life.

Answered Prayers

These milestones are essential to remember as you continue to believe for God's promises to manifest in your life.

_____

_____

_____

_____

_____

_____

_____

_____

_____

_____

Answered Prayers

*These milestones are essential to remember as you continue
to believe for God's promises to manifest in your life.*

_____

_____

_____

_____

_____

_____

_____

_____

_____

_____

Answered Prayers

*These milestones are essential to remember as you continue
to believe for God's promises to manifest in your life.*

_____

_____

_____

_____

_____

_____

_____

_____

_____

_____

Answered Prayers

These milestones are essential to remember as you continue
to believe for God's promises to manifest in your life.

_____

_____

_____

_____

_____

_____

_____

_____

_____

_____

_____

Answered Prayers

These milestones are essential to remember as you continue to believe for God's promises to manifest in your life.

_____

_____

_____

_____

_____

_____

_____

_____

_____

_____

Answered Prayers

These milestones are essential to remember as you continue to believe for God's promises to manifest in your life.

_____

_____

_____

_____

_____

_____

_____

_____

_____

_____

_____

Answered Prayers

These milestones are essential to remember as you continue to believe for God's promises to manifest in your life.

_____

_____

_____

_____

_____

_____

_____

_____

_____

_____

_____

Answered Prayers

*These milestones are essential to remember as you continue
to believe for God's promises to manifest in your life.*

_____

_____

_____

_____

_____

_____

_____

_____

_____

_____

Answered Prayers

These milestones are essential to remember as you continue to believe for God's promises to manifest in your life.

_____

_____

_____

_____

_____

_____

_____

_____

_____

_____

_____

Answered Prayers

These milestones are essential to remember as you continue to believe for God's promises to manifest in your life.

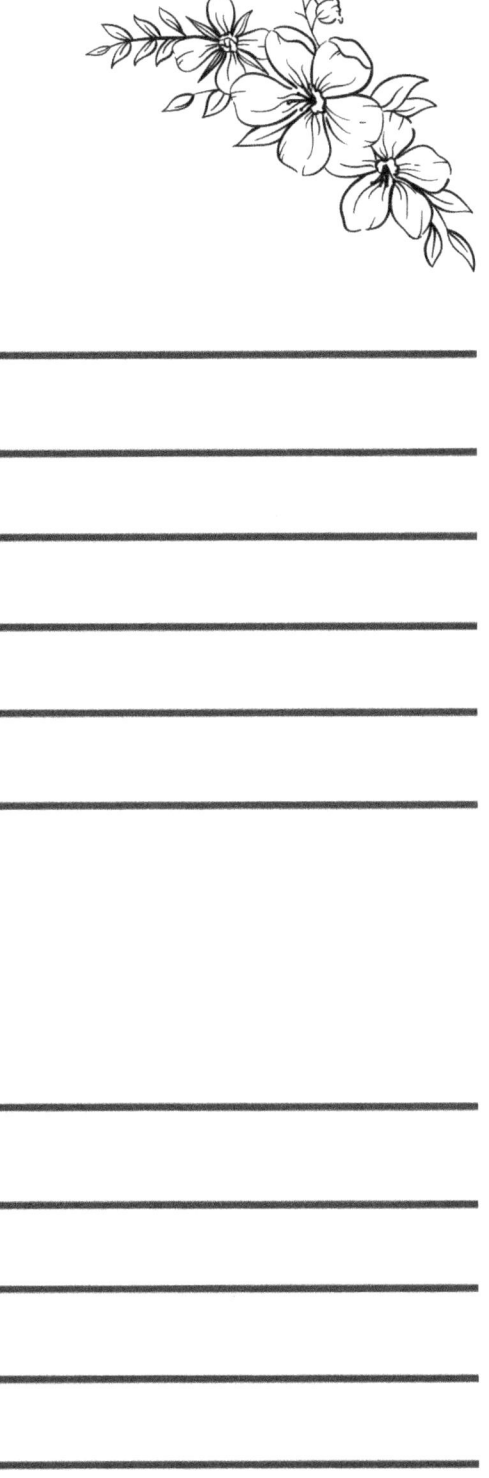

_____

_____

_____

_____

_____

_____

_____

_____

_____

_____

_____

Answered Prayers

These milestones are essential to remember as you continue to believe for God's promises to manifest in your life.

_____

_____

_____

_____

_____

_____

_____

_____

_____

_____

Answered Prayers

These milestones are essential to remember as you continue to believe for God's promises to manifest in your life.

_____

_____

_____

_____

_____

_____

_____

_____

_____

_____

_____

Answered Prayers

These milestones are essential to remember as you continue to believe for God's promises to manifest in your life.

_____

_____

_____

_____

_____

_____

_____

_____

_____

_____

_____

Hey! I'm "Christina"

It is my heart's greatest desire to sit at the feet of Jesus to feast on His Word and enjoy His presence. As a 5-fold minister, revivalist, author, and speaker with a fiery passion for Jesus that spreads like wildfire, I carry the revelation of the gospel of Jesus Christ. I long to bring the body of Christ into the fullness of the finished work of Jesus and see each one of us reach a hurting world with love. It is a great honor to encourage others in the goodness of God.

I sincerely hope this worship and prayer journal has blessed your relationship with God and deepened your walk with Him. I would love to keep in touch and continue encouraging you in the things of God!

We would love to hear how this journal has blessed you. Please leave a review on Amazon to help others know how it has blessed you. You can follow us on social media at @christinapereraministres on Facebook & Instagram. Listen to hear more about our beautiful Savior Jesus on *Revealing Jesus With Christina Perera* wherever you get your podcasts.

LET'S KEEP IN TOUCH